Who Is Ilona Maher?

Who Is Ilona Maher?

by Ellen Labrecque

illustrated by Gregory Copeland

Penguin Workshop

Betsy Laskowski—a rugby player in her own time!—EL

PENGUIN WORKSHOP
An imprint of Penguin Random House LLC
1745 Broadway, New York, NY 10019
penguinrandomhouse.com

Library of Congress Cataloging-in-Publication Data is available.

First published in the United States of America by Penguin Workshop, 2026

Manufactured in the United States of America
CJKW

ISBN 9798217144167 (paperback)
10 9 8 7 6 5 4 3 2 1

ISBN 9798217144174 (library binding)
10 9 8 7 6 5 4 3 2 1

The authorized representative in the EU for product safety and compliance is Penguin Random House Ireland, Morrison Chambers, 32 Nassau Street, Dublin D02 YH68, Ireland, https://eu-contact.penguin.ie.

Contents

Who Is Ilona Maher?

Ilona Maher was in beast mode. The captain and center for the United States women's rugby sevens team had her hair pulled back in stylish braids that led into a ponytail on top of her head. Her lips shone with bright red lipstick. At 5'10", Ilona was tall, strong, and muscular, even for a rugby player. It was July 28, 2024, and her team, called the Eagles, was playing Japan in their opening match at the Summer Olympics in Paris, France.

During the first half of the game, Ilona got her hands on the oval-shaped ball and seized the moment. A defender sprinted toward Ilona to try to stop her. The Eagles center tucked the ball under her muscular right arm and extended her left to stiff-arm the defender. *Boom!* The Japanese player crashed to the ground. Ilona kept sprinting down the field and into the try zone. She scored! The United States dominated for the rest of the match and won, 36–7.

Ilona went on to help her team win the bronze medal at these Games. It was the first time a US rugby team—men's or women's—won an Olympic medal in rugby sevens. On the field after the game, Ilona raised both hands in victory. Then during the medal ceremony later that evening, all of the team, but especially Ilona, cried tears of joy as the medals were placed around their necks.

But Ilona was more than an Olympic medalist: She was also an inspiration to women all over the world thanks to her popular social media posts about self-confidence and her message of celebrating beauty in many different forms. By the Paris Olympics, Ilona had more than eight million followers across Instagram and TikTok who loved her videos about being proud of your muscles, strength, and size. How did this inspirational athlete come to be?

CHAPTER 1
An All-Star Athlete

Ilona Delsing Rosa Maher was born on August 12, 1996, in Burlington, Vermont. Her mom, Mieneke, was a nurse, and her father, Michael, was a dentist. Ilona's older sister, Olivia, was born two years earlier, and her younger sister, Adrianna, was born three years later. The three girls have always been very close, and Ilona calls them her "built-in best friends." The sisters all loved to play sports. Mieneke and Michael believed staying active would help their kids be healthy and gain confidence. They encouraged their daughters to play a different sport every season, including field hockey, basketball, and softball. Ilona always wanted to be on the move, even during the school day. During recess, she spent her time racing around the playground with other active kids. Even at a young age, it was clear that Ilona was great at playing with others. She loved being on a team and working together.

"She picked up things very quickly as a child," said Michael about his daughter's athletic ability. "It was obvious that she really understood the concept of giving and taking space when playing." That understanding made Ilona a great teammate. She knew how to support the

people she was playing with to make them even better.

As she grew up, Ilona became an especially good softball pitcher. In one game, Lo, as her family called her, zipped the ball across the plate so fast that no one could hit it.

A spectator told her to slow her pitches down so the batters could get some hits. Lo's father, who was at the game, told his daughter to do no such thing. Ilona took his words to heart: She decided to never tone herself down to make others more comfortable. Ilona was now determined to always compete as hard as she could, no matter what others said.

Ilona was always tall and big for her age, with broad shoulders and powerful legs and arms. While this made her a great athlete, some classmates, especially boys, would tease her about her size.

"I grew up as big, muscular, and a little chunky," Ilona said. "I always got called manly and masculine by the boys and whatnot and that hurt deeply."

Ilona's parents told their daughter to be proud of her body and who she was. They encouraged her to use her size to be as fast and powerful as possible. Her father told Ilona never to change anything about herself just to please other people.

By her senior year of high school, Ilona had grown tired of playing softball. She wanted a more physical sport where her power and speed would shine. Michael, a former rugby player at Saint Michael's College, suggested Ilona try rugby. A local high school had a rugby club, so Ilona joined. She fell in love with the new sport instantly. Ilona appreciated how physical the game was. Her speed, something she couldn't fully use in softball, became a huge asset in rugby. Her broad shoulders helped her tackle hard. Her strong thighs helped her easily push past opponents. For the sport of rugby, Ilona's size and strength were gifts that made her a better athlete. People praised her body instead of teasing her for it. "The sport fit my body like a glove," she said.

How to Play Rugby

Rugby is a fast-paced physical sport similar to football. But despite its rough nature, the players don't wear pads or helmets!

In the Olympics, teams compete in rugby sevens, with seven players on each side. Other rugby formats, including college competitions and the World Cup, feature teams of fifteen players on each side instead. Rugby sevens matches last fourteen minutes, split into two seven-minute halves. Traditional fifteen-player rugby runs for eighty minutes, with two forty-minute halves.

The games take place on a large grassy field where each team defends its try line (the goal area) while trying to score on their opponent's side. The team with the most points at the end wins the match.

Teams score by carrying, passing, or kicking

an oval-shaped ball (slightly smaller than a football) into the opponent's goal area. Points break down as follows:

- TRY (5 points): A player touches the ball down in the other team's try zone.
- CONVERSION (2 points): After scoring a try, the team kicks the ball through the goalposts.
- PENALTY KICK (3 points): A player kicks the ball through the posts after an opponent commits a foul.
- DROP GOAL (3 points): During open play, a player drops the ball and kicks it through the posts.

Players can run with the ball or pass it backward to teammates—forward passes are not allowed. Tackling must stay below the shoulders. Once tackled, the player must release the ball so others can grab it.

Rugby also has unique terms for different moments in the match.

- SCRUM: A restart after certain fouls where players push against one another to gain possession.
- RUCK: Players fight for the ball on the ground after a tackle.
- MAUL: The ball carrier stays upright while opponents hold them, and teammates push forward to gain ground.

After she had played in just one rugby game, Ilona began receiving calls from college coaches. They saw how naturally talented she was and wanted her on their team. Coaches knew that with more time and experience, Ilona would become an even better player. After graduating high school in 2014, eighteen-year-old Ilona chose to attend Norwich University in Northfield, Vermont, where she joined its rugby sevens team.

CHAPTER 2
The College Years

Ilona thrived as a freshman, or first-year student, at Norwich. In her fifth game, Ilona scored three tries in a 45–38 win over Quinnipiac University in Hamden, Connecticut. Quinnipiac was a nationally ranked team at the time, so their loss to Norwich was considered a major upset. Quinnipiac's coach, Becky Carlson, immediately recognized Ilona's potential as a powerful player.

Around the same time, Ilona realized Norwich wasn't the best fit for her. She wanted to study nursing like her mom and knew Quinnipiac had a strong academic program for that profession. She also wanted to join Quinnipiac's more competitive rugby team—which was a higher-ranked program than Norwich, despite the upset. After Ilona's freshman year, she transferred.

At Quinnipiac, Ilona's rugby skills skyrocketed. She used the field awareness and hand-eye coordination she had gained from all the other sports she had played growing up and excelled.

With the amazing coaches on her new team, Ilona got faster and stronger as she practiced more and more. When she was on the field, she'd run right through opponents rather than around them because her power made her an unstoppable force.

As Ilona's rugby game improved, so did her confidence. She embraced her strong build, understanding it is a gift rather than something to feel self-conscious about.

"I always recognized that my body was really good at sports," she said. "But it wasn't until I played rugby that I learned to love my body."

Ilona also succeeded in the classroom. As a nursing student, she worked twelve-hour shifts in the hospital. She especially enjoyed working in the emergency room setting with its fast-paced energy. Caring for patients, staying on her feet, and working with her hands reminded her of the physical demands of rugby—which she loved.

CHAPTER 3
Going Viral

The Quinnipiac team won national titles every season Ilona played there. As a center, she ran, defended, and passed the ball with ease and natural skill. Off the field, Ilona put in the extra work to get better and better. The team lifted weights at 6:30 a.m. daily and Ilona also trained on her own—pushing herself to be faster and stronger. In 2017, as a junior, she was honored with the MA Sorensen Award as national player of the year, which recognized her as the best women's college rugby player in the United States! This was especially amazing because she had only started playing rugby just a few years before.

At the award ceremony, Coach Carlson made a bold prediction. She told the crowd, "You need to watch Ilona now because you will see her in the Olympics and she is going to be one of the best players in the world."

In just a few years, Ilona's coach would be proven right!

When Ilona graduated from Quinnipiac in 2018, she faced a major crossroads. She loved nursing and considered a career working in the emergency room. But she also wanted to continue playing rugby and compete as a professional athlete. Soon after graduation, Ilona was invited to the Chula Vista Elite Athlete Training Center near San Diego, California. Here, she could try out for the United States women's national rugby team. Ilona asked her nursing professors for advice about what career path to choose. They encouraged her to pursue rugby and reminded her that nursing would always be there, but the chance to compete for an Olympic team would not. This was a once-in-a-lifetime opportunity.

Ilona on her college graduation day

Taking their advice, Ilona flew to San Diego just a week after graduation. She earned her spot on the national team, the Eagles, and began competing internationally. Just one month after her graduation in 2018, Ilona played in the final event of the World Rugby Sevens 2017–2018 series in Paris, France, where the United States finished fifth. The following season, she helped the team secure a second-place overall ranking in the 2018–2019 World Rugby Seven Series. This was the team's best finish ever, and their achievement earned them a spot to compete in the Summer Olympics, scheduled for the summer of 2020 in Tokyo, Japan.

Ilona and her teammates couldn't wait to get to the Olympics! However, in the spring of 2020, coronavirus was rapidly spreading around the world. The virus caused people to get very sick with an illness called COVID-19. COVID-19 was so contagious that the illness was classified as an international pandemic, causing people all over the world to stay indoors and quarantine from areas where they might get sick. Many athletic competitions were shut down or postponed—including the Tokyo Olympics. Officials rescheduled the Games to take place a year later, in the summer of 2021. But because the virus was still circulating, strict safety measures remained in place. Fans would not be allowed to attend, but Ilona refused to let the lack of support in the stands dampen her spirit.

Determined to connect with her fans despite these restrictions, Ilona turned to social media. She posted funny and engaging content on TikTok to introduce herself to a wider audience and to generate enthusiasm for the sport of rugby. With Ilona's lighthearted, authentic, and uplifting posts, often celebrating other athletes—especially women—she gained traction on social media.

Once her team arrived in Tokyo, Ilona's posts became even more popular. She gave viewers an inside look at the Olympic village. She shared footage of the small dorm rooms that the athletes slept in and the communal dining hall,

poking fun of uncomfortable "cardboard" beds and the unfamiliar dining hall food delights. Her TikTok videos made people laugh and feel like they were right there with her, even though they couldn't be because of the pandemic.

Ilona used the hashtag #BeastBeautyBrains to reinforce her message of body positivity and self-love, while also highlighting her skills as an athlete.

"There are so many more dimensions to athletes that aren't talked about," Ilona explained. "I can be a beast on the field, but I think of myself as beautiful. I'm a beauty. I'm smart and I have degrees," she continued. "We're so much more than what we do on the field. I'm so much more than rugby."

Through her words and videos, Ilona showed that she and her teammates weren't just aggressive rugby players—they possessed other talents and strengths. Every post carried a positive vibe—celebrating all athletes rather than tearing anyone down. Ilona's content quickly went viral, racking up millions of views.

"Social media became a great tool to get myself, my team, and my sport out there," Ilona said. Spreading the word was important to her because she and her teammates were trying to grow the game of rugby around the world, but especially in America, where rugby is not as popular as other professional sports.

The US women's rugby team finished sixth in the Games and Ilona scored three tries during the competition. Even though her team didn't win a medal in Tokyo, Ilona had been a standout and quickly became rugby's top star.

With her Olympic debut behind her, Ilona hoped to compete in the next Games, which would be held in Paris during the summer of 2024. More than anything else, she wanted the opportunity to have her family and friends in the stands, cheering her on.

CHAPTER 4
The Paris Olympics

Ilona felt a little down after the Tokyo Games ended. She had trained for so many years, only to have it come to an end so quickly. The time period after the Games felt like such a low, after experiencing such an Olympic high. Ilona reached out to a therapist, a person who helps a patient identify and change troubling emotions and behaviors, to work through these feelings. The therapist helped her get back a healthier attitude. Thanks to that help, Ilona was able to look back on the Tokyo Olympics and be proud of what she had accomplished. But now it was time to start working toward her next goal. She would train hard and compete on the national team, while also getting her message out to the world on social media.

In September 2022, Ilona helped lead her team to the semifinals at the 2022 Rugby World Cup Sevens in Cape Town, South Africa.

She also continued to post on TikTok. Every post was funny and silly, but also heartfelt. She posted about rugby and how hard she was still practicing and working. But she also posted about something as simple as what she was eating for breakfast—which was such an important source of fuel for an Olympic athlete. Other times she shared her honest struggles, like the times where she didn't feel as comfortable in her "bigger body." Sometimes, she would be very bold and use internet trolls—people who post mean or rude things with the intent of upsetting others—as motivation. If somebody posted that they thought she ate too much, she would simply say something such as "I have a bigger body, so I need more food to fuel it and be the best I can be."

In March 2023, Ilona faced the biggest setback of her career. She broke her ankle in a touch rugby game during practice against a men's team, and would require surgery to heal. She had never struggled with such a major injury in her sport before. But she confronted it the way she tackled every challenge—head-on, sharing the painful journey with fans.

Ilona posted updates about her surgery and her recovery time. In one post she worked out in the gym all alone with an ankle brace on her foot. She admitted that recovery wasn't easy, but she was committed to doing whatever it took to return to the pitch. She showed that injuries happen in sports, but that athletes can put in the work to heal and come back stronger.

As an adult, Ilona was still very close with her sisters and her mom and dad. Olivia, Ilona's older sister, became her publicity manager to help Ilona come up with new videos and content for her social media. Ilona's whole family supported her as she recovered from her injury and helped her in any way they could.

Eight months passed, and by November 2023, Ilona was back on the field, helping the Eagles win a gold medal in the women's rugby sevens at the nineteenth Pan American Games, held in Santiago, Chile. It was the first gold for the US women's rugby sevens team in the competition's history. After this big win, the team couldn't wait to compete in the Olympics the following summer.

The 2024 Summer Olympics were held in Paris. Ilona and her teammates didn't want to finish in sixth place like they had last time—they wanted to win a medal.

The US women's rugby team became fan favorites at the Games, and much of that enthusiasm was thanks to Ilona's positive personality. In every match, Ilona wore her signature bright red lipstick, making a statement and catching attention.

"I believe rugby is a very physical game," Ilona said. "But I also think you don't have to sacrifice your femininity or your beauty by playing it."

People were also tuning in because the American team was so good, and that made them very fun to watch. Jason Kelce, a former NFL player for the Philadelphia Eagles, became one of the team's biggest fans. During games, Jason sported a shirt with a pattern of Ilona's face all over it. Jason supported the US women's rugby team by going to many of their games and filming funny videos with them. In one video, Jason arm-wrestled several of the incredibly strong women on the team.

And just as in Tokyo, Ilona continued to make social media posts. In her posts, Ilona didn't just promote rugby, she also supported other athletes, such as gymnast Simone Biles and swimmer Katie Ledecky. One of her most important and popular posts was about Olympic body types. "All body types matter, all body types are worthy," Ilona said, "from the smallest gymnast to the tallest water polo player." Ilona gave the following advice to her young viewers: "All body types are beautiful and can do amazing things, so truly see yourself in these athletes and know that you can do it, too."

The US women's rugby team beat Great Britain, 17–7, in the Olympic quarterfinals, but then lost to New Zealand, 12–24, in their semifinal match. This meant they would have to face Australia to compete for the bronze. If they didn't win, they'd go home without a medal. The match was played in front of 69,000 fans in ninety-degree heat. Team USA scored a try with only seconds left to tie the game and then scored on a conversion to win, 14–12.

They went home with the first medal for USA rugby sevens—men or women—since the sport was added in 2016. Ilona and her teammates had made history.

CHAPTER 5
The Bristol Bears

Following the Paris Olympics, Ilona's fame surged. Journalists and fans nicknamed her America's Sweetheart. This is a term for a famous person who is beloved and admired by the American people. Ilona was honored by this nickname. She loved that she was a role model for kids out there, especially young girls. She soon had more than eight million social media followers across all platforms. This was the most followers of any rugby player in the world.

Ilona was up front about her reasons for being so active on social media. Sure, it was fun and it helped promote the sport of rugby, but she was also able to make some money through her posts. Even though rugby is an Olympic sport and Ilona was a professional athlete, she did not make a lot of money as a rugby player. However, her social media stardom helped supplement her income in other ways. Ilona, like a lot of women athletes, had to work very hard both on and off the pitch so that she could afford to pursue her rugby dreams. Many women in sports are not paid very much to play, even if they are Olympic medalists and champions. This has been a problem for many decades.

Ilona had earned a master's degree in business administration from DeVry University in 2022 that helped her learn about how she could earn money through her social media posts by collaborating with different companies. She became the face and spokesperson of brands like Quaker Oats, Coppertone, and Adidas, appearing in advertisements and endorsing products. Ilona also created her own brand—Beast Beauty Brains—that encouraged female athletes to embrace all their great qualities. Her brand sold shirts, and the proceeds went to supporting girls' rugby teams.

In November 2024, Ilona made history by competing in the thirty-third season of *Dancing with the Stars*—the first rugby player of any gender ever to do so. She became the first woman to lift a male partner when she held up Alan Bersten. Ilona admitted that, unlike rugby, dancing did not come easy to her. She even broke down in tears on one of the shows when she struggled with a routine that required fast-paced footwork. But she kept working hard and made her message clear about why she was dancing on the show in the first place—"for all the girls who've been told they're too big or they're too muscular and they're not pretty," she said.

Ilona improved every week and became a talented dancer over the course of the show. She and Alan finished in second place overall.

Dancing with the Stars was not the only

opportunity that came Ilona's way. She was asked to pose for the cover of *Sports Illustrated* and she appeared on countless television talk shows. More brands wanted her to appear in their advertisements. After the Olympics, Ilona's jersey became the most popular rugby jersey in the world, and it outsold all the men's jerseys. Her agent had trouble keeping up with the flood of requests from people who wanted to work with Ilona.

Despite her busy schedule, Ilona longed to be back on the rugby field. In January 2025, she joined the Bristol Bears in the Premiership Women's Rugby league. Her contract with the Bears was only for a few months. Ilona's team was based about a hundred miles from London. The league is the best women's rugby league in the world because rugby is a much more popular sport in the United Kingdom than it is in the United States. Ilona said she loved being in a country that loved her sport just as she did. Unlike Ilona's league in the United States, the Premiership league was played with fifteen players on each side, with each match lasting eighty minutes. This meant Ilona would have to train even harder than before to maintain her endurance during the longer game time. In the United States, her matches were only fourteen minutes! Ilona wanted to get comfortable playing in this format in preparation for the 2025 World Cup the following summer.

Right after Ilona signed with Bristol, the Bears moved her first game to a bigger stadium to accommodate all the fans who wanted to see her play. More than nine thousand spectators came to the game—a single-game record for the entire league. After the match, Ilona spent a lot of time with fans who looked up to her and wanted to meet her. Ilona was thrilled to interact with all the people who came to watch her games. She was often surprised when people cried tears of joy when they got to meet her. It meant a lot to her that people cared so much.

Ilona played for three months in Bristol. She scored four tries in seven league matches (regular season games). Her team lost in the Premiership semifinal game (the playoffs) to Gloucester-Hartpury in front of more than seven thousand fans. Bristol coach Dave Ward was thrilled to have Ilona on his team. "She put us on the map," Dave said. "The energy that she brought to the squad is exactly what we needed at the time."

Ilona brings positive energy wherever she goes—and perhaps that is why people all over the world want to support her. In March 2025, the athletic clothing company Adidas recognized this energy and signed Ilona to a multiyear partnership. They made a signature rugby cleat for her—black with sparkles—the perfect beast and beauty combination. This was the first time they had ever done this for a woman rugby player.

After playing in Bristol, Ilona headed back to the United States to start training with the national team for the 2025 Women's Rugby World Cup, set to take place in eight venues across England. The World Cup is held every four years. It is contested by sixteen international teams. The Eagles won the gold medal in the first-ever women's World Cup rugby tournament in 1991 and claimed silver in 1994 and 1998, but they hadn't finished in the top three since before Ilona was born. Ilona is working very hard to get her team back to the medal stand—just like she did at the Olympics.

In March 2025, Ilona and her sisters, Olivia and Adrianna, launched a new podcast called *House of Maher*. The podcast features the sisters chatting, having fun, and giving advice to listeners. Ilona said that as she became more famous, family time became hard to come by, so she appreciates being able to spend time with her sisters as they record their podcast episodes.

The next Olympics are in Los Angeles, California, in 2028, and Ilona is hoping to be on the team again. She is already working hard to make her dream a reality. Ilona is also still committed to creating positive content on social media to inspire young people. She has admitted that she never intended to be a role model for young girls, but she is still very grateful for the impact she has made.

Ilona continues to uplift women's rugby and women athletes all over the world through her social media posts. She also continues to encourage self-confidence in young people by teaching them to love their bodies no matter how big or small they are. Because of Ilona, many people from all over the world have been able to celebrate their own strength and power.

"I don't think I started my funny little videos to change lives but I guess that's what they have done for some," Ilona reflected. "I just like sharing myself with you all and showing that it's okay to exist as you are, whether that be strong, loud, funny, quiet, shy . . ."

Ilona has said that, above all, her goal is always to support women and cheer them on as they pursue their passions and dreams. And that's exactly what she has done and continues to do.

Timeline of Ilona Maher's Life

1996 — Ilona Delsing Rosa Maher is born on August 12

2013 — Begins playing rugby for a local high school club team

2014 — Starts at Norwich University and plays on their rugby team

2015 — Transfers to Quinnipiac University, where she wins three national championships

2017 — Wins the MA Sorensen Award, which is given to the nation's top collegiate women's rugby player

2018 — Makes her debut on the United States women's national team at a tournament in Paris, France

2021 — Competes at the Olympics in Tokyo, Japan, where she helps lead Team USA to a sixth-place finish

2024 — Leads Team USA to the bronze medal at the Olympics in Paris, France

— Competes on *Dancing with the Stars* and finishes in second place

2025 — Makes her official debut with the Bristol Bears in the Premiership Women's Rugby league in England

— Reaches more than eight million combined followers on Instagram and TikTok

Timeline of the World

1996	The United States wins the most medals (101) at the Olympics in Atlanta, Georgia
2001	Terrorists hijack four planes, crashing two into the World Trade Center on September 11
2014	Basketball player Jason Collins comes out, becoming the first openly gay athlete to play in the NBA
2015	The US Supreme Court legalizes same-sex marriage nationwide
2017	Hundreds of thousands of women descend on the National Mall in Washington, DC, to express support for women's rights
2018	Meghan Markle marries Prince Harry on May 19
2020	The COVID-19 coronavirus pandemic causes much of the globe to go into lockdown to stop the spread of the virus
2021	Joe Biden is sworn in as president of the United States
2024	The year goes down as the hottest year ever on record
2025	The Women's Rugby World Cup takes place from August 22 to September 27 in eight venues across England

Bibliography

Abrami, Alex. "She Did It, It's Her Dedication: How Ilona Maher Turned into an Olympian." ***Burlington Free Press***, July 22, 2021. https://www.burlingtonfreepress.com/in-depth/sports/2021/07/22/ilona-maher-burlington-vermont-quinnipiac-usa-rugby-team-olympics-roster/7872927002/.

Ainsworth, Imogen. "Ilona Maher Becomes Rugby's Most Followed Player on Instagram." Rugbypass. July 28, 2024. https://www.rugbypass.com/news/ilona-maher-becomes-most-followed-current-rugby-player-on-instagram/#:~:text=USA%20sevens%20star%20and%20social,both%20have%201.3%20million%20followers.

Ishmael, Aiyana. "Rugby Olympian and Social Media Star Ilona Maher Was Made for This." ***Teen Vogue***, July 27, 2024. https://www.teenvogue.com/story/rugby-olympian-and-social-media-star-ilona-maher-was-made-for-this.

O'Neill, Caoimhe. "Ilona Maher and the Sisterhood Fuelling a Women's Sport Trailblazer." ***The Athletic***, March 8, 2025. https://www.nytimes.com/athletic/6180792/2025/03/08/ilona-maher-rugby-olympics-family/.

Plank, Liz. "Beast. Beauty. Brains." ***Sports Illustrated***, September 2024.

Websites

usa.rugby

www.world.rugby